Prayers for L

SUSAN SAYERS

With Open Arms

First published in 1996 by
KEVIN MAYHEW LTD
Rattlesden
Bury St Edmunds
Suffolk IP30 0SZ

ISBN 0 86209 832 7
Catalogue No 1500070

0 1 2 3 4 5 6 7 8 9

Cover photograph courtesy of Tony Stone Images

Design by Veronica Ward
Artwork by Graham Johnstone

Edited by Peter Dainty
Typesetting by Louise Hill
Printed and bound in Great Britain

CONTENTS

God's Love and Ours

Lord, as our love
    for one another grows,
    keep us rooted
    firmly and deeply
    in your unending love.

And as we each
    grow closer to you,
    draw us closer
    to one another.

When we are totally at one,
   spent and fulfilled
   in one another,

   your love, O God, pervades us.

When tempers flare
   and reconciliation is costly,

   your love, O God, restores us.

When illness and frailty
   disrupt our hopes and plans,

   your love, O God, sustains us.

Isn't it strange, Lord,
    how you can spend time
    with someone you love
    and not need to speak,
    necessarily, at all.

And yet the communication
    is powerful and deep.

It is as if we are wrapped up
    in a cloth of affection
    woven with colours
    we both enjoy,
    warm to the touch
    but unrestricting –
    like your love to us
    which holds us
    yet enables us to be free.

God of love,
    teach me to love
    the way you love.

Teach me the love
    I can promise with my will;
    the love which
    doesn't rely on feelings;
    the love which is not reliant
    on mutual attraction
    or warm response;

    the love that reaches out
    without demanding
    emotional feedback;
    the love that
    sets self down
    and rolls up its sleeves
    for action.

MARRIAGE

Lord of our provision,
   if it is your will,
   I ask you to provide for me
   a marriage partner.

After all, you know me
   and understand my needs
   and what I can give
   better than anyone,
   and I know you love me.

So I entrust to you
   this deep desire and need I feel
   and ask you to hear my request.

If the single life
   would enable me better to serve you,
   then so be it;
   but if not,
   would you introduce me
   to someone whom I could love,
   and who would love me,
   so that we could marry
   and raise a family?

Lord, I stood at the door
   and watched
   this woman, my wife,
   walking down the street
   with our child.

She didn't know I was watching.
They were talking together
   and smiling.
She was beautiful.

I love her so much
   for all that she is to me.

Loving God
   we dedicate ourselves afresh
   to one another
   and to you.

On this, our anniversary,
   we call to mind
   the journey we have travelled together
   the dark and sunlit places,
   the storms and the havens.

Thank you, Lord God,
   for your loving,
   your faithfulness
   within ours.

Once more we commit ourselves
   to love and to cherish,
   within the arch
   of your cherishing.

MAKING FRIENDS

Lord, if only
   I had a friend,
   someone to talk to,
   who'd be pleased
   when I popped in;
   someone to listen;
   someone who would
   share their thoughts with me.

You say, 'Ask anything
   in my name . . .'

Is it OK
   if I ask for a friend?

Forgive me, Lord,
    I did far too much talking
    and missed out on the listening.

I think I was scared
    of there being long silences
    so I filled up all the gaps.

But there need to be a few spaces;
    time to think.

Give me the courage next time
    to welcome the patches of silence
    for our friendship
    to take root in
    and grow.

It's strange, Lord,
    how we sometimes set out
    thinking we're doing the good deed
    and end up being receivers.

To be honest,
    I wasn't looking forward
    to visiting this elderly neighbour
    and I did it, feeling noble.

How wrong can you be!
I really look forward to those visits now.

She ensures that I sit down
    and I relax and listen
    to her wonderful stories
    from a completely different world
    I was born too late to inhabit.

It's quality time
    and I am really thankful
    for our friendship.

What do you think, Jesus;
    is this a valuable friendship
    or is it the beginning
    of a dangerous relationship?

I suppose the fact that I'm asking
    says it all –
    there must be something
    that makes me uneasy,
    even though nothing explicit
    has ever been said.

Protect us from evil, O God,
    and lead us not into temptation.

Remind me of all my family
    whom I love and hold so dear.

And thank you
    for showing me warning lights
    in time to avoid the danger.

THE JOYS OF FRIENDSHIP

Thank you, my Lord,
   for that phone call
   from my friend.

Just when I needed
   cheering up
   she rang
   and cheered me up.

Just when I needed
   to see the funny side of things
   she showed it to me
   and we ended up laughing.

What a gift!
Thank you, my Lord.

Loving God,
  bless our time together today,
  as we talk over memories,
  catch up on news
  and put the world to rights.

It seems no time at all
  since we were students,
  sharing our lives' secrets,
  and the kitchen
  and our dreams.

Thank you for our friendship
  over the years
  and all it has given us.

Two friends
    sharing a drink together
    after work.

A joke or two.
A wry telling of the day's woe.

The tensions slide away
    and it truly feels like
    re-creation, my Lord.

You were right,
    we do need one another.

I praise and thank you
    for your wholesome provision
    of mutual comfort and renewing
    in a good friendship.

There is something
    particularly special
    about celebrating together
    with a shared meal –
    the food and drink,
    the conversations,
    the looking after
    one another's needs.

And as we gather
    at the sharing of your feast,
    and you feed us
    and you quench our thirst,
    supplying our needs,
    the harmony and love among us
    grow and mellow
    in your peace.

I am going to miss
    these people, Lord,
    after spending a week
    on holiday together.

You get so close,
    sharing meals and jokes
    and difficulties
    and worship.

I suppose we have grown
    from a group of individuals
    into a community.

Perhaps we have grown
    into more of a church,
    with mutual concern,
    brotherly and sisterly love.

Let this not be lost
    as we go home, Lord,
    but use it
    for the good of the world.

My two year old and I
   lingered over a feast
   of Smarties today.

We sorted the colours,
   and tried eating them
   fastest and slowest,
   and I gave to her
   from my pile
   and she gave to me
   from hers.

And, Lord, we weren't only
   mother and daughter.
We were friends.

Lord, I want to thank you
   for my doggy friend here,
   grinning away in his doggy way,
   tail thrashing!

What would a muddy walk
   be without him?
What would coming home be
   without his wet and lavish welcome?

It's a very special
   doggy/human friendship
   we enjoy!

STRENGTH IN WEAKNESS

Father, I want to thank you
   for the extraordinary
   outpouring of love
   I have experienced
   through being ill.
People are so kind!

It isn't just the cards
   and flowers
   (which really helped,
   and lifted my spirits),
   but it's also the expression
   in their eyes,
   the praying for me
   when I couldn't pray myself;
   the being there
   and standing alongside.

It was your love
   I was experiencing,
   wasn't it, Lord?
Your amazing love!

The love you weave around us,
   loving Lord,
   is so sustaining and strong
   and helps us to bear
   what otherwise
   would be beyond our bearing.

I could not pray as I struggled for life,
   but was aware of the
   love and prayers of many
   good and faithful friends
   upholding me
   with that network of your love.

Damaged Relationships

When we were laughing
    and joking together
    it just felt like a good time.

But now, Lord,
    thinking it over,
    I can see that it got out of hand
    and more than a bit unkind.
Perhaps it's not surprising,
    after all,
    that one of them
    left, upset.

I'm sorry.
I want to put things right.
Give me the opportunity
    to apologise
    and sort it out.

Lord my God,
   I come to you in sadness
   knowing that I have let
   my good friend down.

I know she is hurt
   and upset by my absence
   and I have no excuse.
Being busy
   is really no excuse.

Perhaps I should look at my life,
   at my priorities.
If I haven't enough time
   for my friends when they need me,
   what are my values?

Help me sort this important
   question out, Lord God.
Show me what needs to change.

It hurts to be let down
    by your friends,
    doesn't it, Lord.

The more you trusted them
    the worse it feels.

My gut reaction
    is never
    to trust anyone
    ever again.

I'll tell you another thing though –
    I've never valued your faithfulness
    so much as I do now.

O Lord,
   if I didn't love him so much
   it wouldn't hurt so much.
I could simply shrug my shoulders
   and ignore him.

But as it is
   I do love him – dearly.

So help me to reach out again
   and start the healing.

Jesus, Our Friend

Jesus, friend of sinners,
   friend of publicans,
   tax collectors and prostitutes,
   friend of outcasts,
   friend of the despised,
   friend of the ineffective and the
      inadequate,
   friend of prisoners,
   friend of traitors,
be my friend,
   and give me the grace
   to reach out
   to your other friends
   in an open,
   two-way friendship.

Being your friend, Jesus,
    certainly doesn't make
    for a dull life.

Just when I think
    I'm getting the hang of things,
    you call me on
    to a new situation.

Just when I'm
    beginning to think
    you've gone without me,
    I find you at my side.

Lead on, my friend;
    this journey
    may not be club class travel,
    but it's the only way
    for me!

If I were you, my Lord,
   I would probably have
   given up on me, by now.

Thank you, my Lord,
   for forgiving
   again and again and again.

Thank you for using
   each tangled mess
   I present you with,
   in some strange way,
   for good.

You are indeed
   faithful
   and of great mercy.